This book is officially licensed by Winning Moves UK Ltd, owners of the Top Trumps registered trademark.

Transformers © 2007 Hasbro. All rights reserved.
© 2007 Dream Works LLC and Paramount Pictures Corporation.
Pave Low, Sikorsky and the Pave Low helicopter design is used under license from Sikorsky Aircraft Corporation. Camaro © General Motors. Pontiac Solstice © General Motors. Hummer H2 © General Motors. Topkick © General Motors. Saleen and S281 © Saleen Inc. LOCKHEED MARTIN, F-22 Raptor © Lockheed Martin Corp. Buffalo MPCV © Force Protection Industries.

Simon Furman has asserted his right to be identified as the author of this book.

British Library Cataloguing-in-Publication Data:
A catalogue record for this book is available from the British Library

ISBN 978 1 84425 502 3

Library of Congress catalog card no. 2007934635

Published by Haynes Publishing,
Sparkford, Yeovil, Somerset BA22 7JJ, UK
Tel: +44 (0)1963 442030 Fax: +44 (0)1963 440001
Email: sales@haynes.co.uk Website: www.haynes.co.uk

Haynes North America, Inc.,
861 Lawrence Drive, Newbury Park, California 91320, USA

Printed and bound in Great Britain by J. H. Haynes & Co. Ltd, Sparkford

The Author

Simon Furman is a writer for comic books and TV animation, his name inextricably linked to Transformers. He has written hundreds of stories about the war-torn 'robots in disguise', and is the author of several other books on Transformers.

CONTENTS

ABOUT
TOP TRUMPS

It's now more than 30 years since Britain's kids first caught the Top Trumps craze. The game remained hugely popular until the 1990s, when it slowly drifted into obscurity. Then, in 1999, UK games company Winning Moves discovered it, bought it, dusted it down, gave it a thorough makeover and introduced it to a whole new generation. And so the Top Trumps legend continues.

Nowadays, there are Top Trumps titles for just about everyone, with subjects about animals, cars, ships, aircraft and all the great films and TV shows. Top Trumps is now even more popular than before. In Britain, a pack of Top Trumps is bought every six seconds! And it's not just British children who love the game. Children in Australasia, the Far East, the Middle East, all over Europe and in North America can buy Top Trumps at their local shops.

Today you can even play the game on the internet, interactive DVD, your games console and even your mobile phone.

YOU'VE PLAYED THE GAME...

NOW READ THE BOOK!

Haynes Publishing and Top Trumps have teamed
up to bring you this exciting new Top Trumps book,
in which you will find even more pictures, facts and
vital statistics.

Top Trumps: Transformers features 28 key characters
from the 2007 film *Transformers*. This is the essential
pocket guide, covering Autobots and Decepticons plus
human characters from the hit movie, which is based on
the toy phenomenon of the 1980s.

Look out for other Top Trumps books from Haynes
Publishing – even more facts, even more fun!

OPTIMUS PRIME

AUTOBOT

As leader of the heroic Autobots, Optimus Prime combines both strength and compassion, wherever possible striving to resolve disputes swiftly and painlessly. When diplomacy and reason fail, though, Prime is a towering and proficient warrior with a staggering array of offensive options on tap and a unique and visionary approach to battle tactics. To keep the awesomely powerful All Spark from Megatron's clutches, Optimus Prime launched it into the far reaches of outer space, knowing full well that in doing so he was dooming Cybertron. When it became clear that Megatron would never give up his search, Prime ordered his Autobot forces to begin their own search for the All Spark, one that led—many, many years later—to Earth. In robot form, Prime's hyper-coil musculature and cobalt super-alloy armour make him both incredibly strong and highly resistant to injury. Prime can call upon remote-access drone units for an instant, multi-aspect battlefield overview.

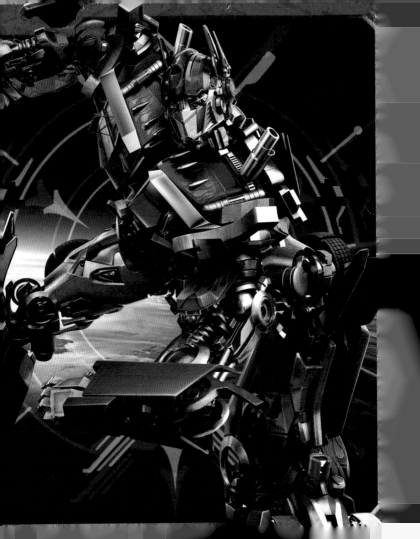

OPTIMUS PRIME

AUTOBOT

On arrival on Earth, Optimus Prime abandoned his (protoform) 'comet' configuration and adopted the vehicular likeness of a deluxe six-wheel drive semi-truck. His revolutionary slow-burn engine continually recycles expended fuel, adding hundreds of miles to his overall combat range, and though built more for endurance than speed, when he needs to accelerate rapidly he can draw on a concentrated well of emergency power stored in compacted energy cells on either flank. His vehicle mode is equipped with thirty-nine independent artillery muzzles and roof-mounted surface-to-air missile launchers with plasma-burn payloads. Enemy entrenchments and siege defences prove little obstacle to Prime when he is fully rolling, and often he'll lead the charge, clearing a path for the ground troops. Transformation to and from vehicle/robot mode takes just four point six seconds, and in robot mode Prime's weapon of choice becomes his laser-sighted barrage cannon.

OPTIMUS PRIME

AUTOBOT

STATISTICS

Alternative Mode	Modified Peterbilt Semi-truck
Function	Autobot Leader
Rank	Commander-in-chief
Height	8.5m
Weight	4.3 tonnes
Power Level	5
Max. Speed	250mph
Engine	850hp
Primary Weapon	Barrage Cannon
Sector 7 Threat Rating	10

'Freedom is
the right of all
sentient beings'

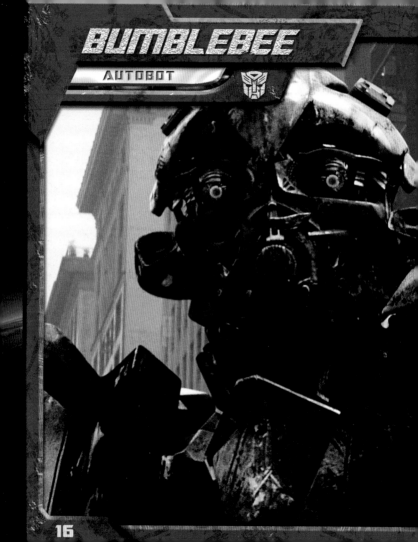

BUMBLEBEE

AUTOBOT

BUMBLEBEE

AUTOBOT

Intrepid, determined, loyal – these are all qualities
Bumblebee possesses in abundance. Not that he
necessarily follows orders blindly, but when it comes
to duty Bumblebee will always see the job through to
the bitter end and get it done. Though perhaps not
one of the most powerful Autobots, where Bumblebee
doesn't physically measure up, he more than compensates
with his sheer tenacity and the great well of resourcefulness
he brings to the table. Most of all, Bumblebee believes
wholeheartedly in Optimus Prime and the fundamental
necessity of their rearguard action against the
Decepticons. That makes him willing to go the
extra distance, to put others before himself, and,
if necessary, make the ultimate sacrifice. No
wonder Optimus Prime entrusts him with the
most crucial and exacting missions. In robot
mode, Bumblebee is fast and manoeuvrable,
making him a difficult target, and he can
focus all his internal reserves of power
into one 'super-surge' attack.

BUMBLEBEE

AUTOBOT

Possessing little or no vanity or image consciousness, Bumblebee cared little (beyond its functionality and disguise potential) what local form he adopted when he arrived on Earth. Thus, he opted for a make and model of Chevy Camaro that had, let's say, seen better days. It was only when it was pointed out to him that a more updated and therefore higher performance model was available to him that he upgraded to a brand spanking new Concept Camaro. With stealth glass, solar receptors/emitters and rear targeting sights, not to mention an array of micro-mines and concussive flash grenades, he was well and truly ready for the battle ahead. Though his Solar Accelerator weapon is only accessible in robot mode, in vehicle mode Bumblebee can generate a chassis-wide solar flare that overloads robotic sensors and knocks out surveillance equipment. Bumblebee specializes in hit-and-run tactics, adopting a fast zig-zag approach to enemy entrenchments.

BUMBLEBEE

AUTOBOT

STATISTICS

Alternative Mode	Chevy Camaro GTO
Function	Special Ops
Rank	Captain
Height	4.9m
Weight	1.6 tonnes
Power Level	2
Max. Speed	230mph
Engine	450hp
Primary Weapon	Solar Accelerator
Sector 7 Threat Rating	6

'Who's gonna drive you home?'

IRONHIDE

AUTOBOT

Often referred to, though not to his face, as Optimus Prime's "big stick", Ironhide is about as far from subtle as you can get. His level of battle strategy amounts to "charge!" and you'll often find him at the forefront of any offensive, head lowered, storming enemy positions. It's just as well he's one of the toughest and most durable Autobots of all, and doesn't seem to mind that odd bits get blown off here and there. Ironhide's taciturn nature masks a deep and abiding concern for his fellow Autobots. He'd willingly lay down his life if it meant others make it out alive, but in the end he's just too tough and too stubborn to die. Though he carries a large amount of heavy artillery, including his radial missile launcher and fission cannon (which combine to form one colossal mega-bazooka), Ironhide prefers to see the colour-filters in his opponents' optics before he engages.

IRONHIDE

AUTOBOT

Though modelled on a GMC Top Kick pickup truck, Ironhide's Earth form is more akin to a tank, with its heavy-duty armour plating and thundering, nigh-on unstoppable forward momentum. Big, bold and utterly all-terrain, his vehicular form is very much a statement of intent. Solid-mould mud-grappler tyres, load-bearing bed and hi-jacked suspension make for a fairly unstoppable force, and if you're the immovable object, the wise move would be to get out of the way. If need be, Ironhide can carry three times his own weight, and his rear section is multi-function, becoming everything from a troop carrier to a fuel truck when augmented with custom cage sections. His robot mode weapons are stored under the main chassis, below the driver and passenger doors, and can be rolled out and fired even in motion. An in-built strobe feature makes it difficult for anyone to get a solid target lock on Ironhide.

STATISTICS

Alternative Mode	Gmc Top Kick Pick-up
Function	Tactical
Rank	Lieutenant
Height	6.8m
Weight	3.8 tonnes
Power Level	3
Max. Speed	180mph
Engine	500hp
Primary Weapon	Mega-bazooka
Sector 7 Threat Rating	7

'I'm comin' through!'

JAZZ

AUTOBOT

JAZZ

AUTOBOT

Jazz possesses style and substance in great abundance. One of the most adaptable and naturally inquisitive of all the Autobots, Jazz is exactly what you need on a mission to an alien world, especially one where you need to blend in – fast. He absorbs facts and figures like a sponge, assimilating language, culture and geo-political data at a staggering rate, tapping into all the local information highways and relaying the essentials to his fellow Autobots. Jazz is also a great facilitator, making things happen and getting you exactly what you need for the job at hand. On the battlefield he's a very cool customer, and no matter how tight the spot, he still manages to assess, collate and feed tactical information right to where it's needed. In robot mode, Jazz can access microfine sensor net in his armour, analysing atmospheric and environmental conditions. This, combined with his analytical visor, means nothing escapes his attention.

JAZZ

AUTOBOT

Jazz is very fast, both in robot and vehicle mode. He's also somewhat picky when it comes to selecting a vehicular mode, immediately seeking out the high-performance end of the market. In other words, if it isn't sporty, pricey and guaranteed to turn heads, he doesn't want to know. Where Bumblebee clearly doesn't, Jazz wholly appreciates the difference between what's functional... and what's cool! On Earth, he adopted the form of a silver '07 Pontiac Solstice, which fulfilled all his rigorous requirements. Equipped with a cryo-emitter weapon, hich issues directional jets of freezing liquid nitrogen, his vehicle mode also as a friction-retardant surface that increases his land speed. The trouble is, Jazz ends to be a little over-protective of his bodywork, diverting the low level forcefield that protects his Spark core to fend off the odd dent or scratch. Given a choice, he'd rather fight the good fight in robot mode.

JAZZ

AUTOBOT

STATISTICS

Alternative Mode	Pontiac Solstice
Function	Cultural Attache
Rank	First Lieutentant
Height	4.7m
Weight	1.8 tonnes
Power Level	2
Max. Speed	400mph
Engine	450hp
Primary Weapon	Cryo-emitter
Sector 7 Threat Rating	6

'Do it with style'

RATCHET

AUTOBOT

RATCHET

AUTOBOT

Strong, decisive and level headed, Ratchet is far more than your average field medic. Sure, he's all about saving lives. It's what, first and foremost, he does, but that's barely scratching the surface of this quiet, highly motivated deep thinker. For a start, there's almost nowhere he won't go, no place he fears to tread. The more problematic a search/rescue situation is, the tougher or more inaccessible the terrain, the more Ratchet likes it. In his mind, there's no obstacle that can't be overcome, no mountain that can't be moved. That mindset aids him immensely in his other role, as chief negotiator and diplomat. Ratchet navigates these equally treacherous realms with consummate ease. In robot mode, Ratchet carries a wide range of welding, freezing and cutting tools, as well as a number of redundant (internal) systems that he can cannibalize for patients in the field. His bi-directional wrist-mounted cutters double as a weapon for close combat.

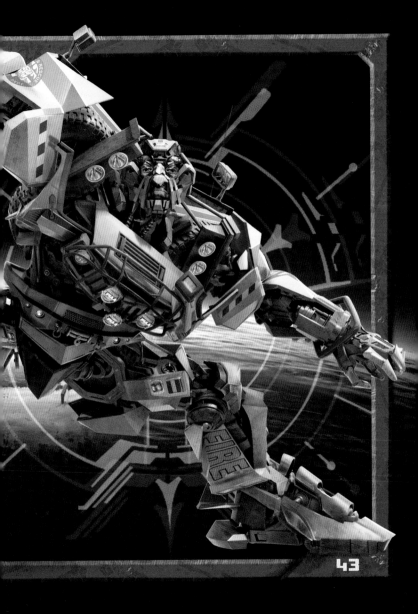

RATCHET

Ratchet is built for strength, not speed, and his vehicular mode (on Earth, a Hummer H2 emergency search/rescue vehicle) is all about getting there and getting the job done. His ultra-durable, heavy-duty armature and forward ramming bars (moulded metal/silicate amalgam) mean he tends to go through (rather than around) obstacles. Special all-terrain tyres with a retractable traction stud layer, ensure that no matter what the ground's like, or how wet and muddy things get, he never gets stuck. Ratchet can haul or push over twenty times his own weight, using a vibrational force distribution system located under his main chassis. Often, enemies assume that because Ratchet is sworn to protect and preserve life and limb, he's unwilling to really let loose in a battle situation. They're wrong. In either vehicular or robot mode, Ratchet is more than willing to take on anything or anyone in a combat situation, even Megatron!

RATCHET

AUTOBOT

STATISTICS

Alternative Mode	Hummer H2
Function	Medic
Rank	Captain
Height	6.1m
Weight	6.7 tonnes
Power Level	4
Max. Speed	230mph
Engine	650hp
Primary Weapon	Bi-directional Cutters
Sector 7 Threat Rating	5

'Self-belief can move mountains'

THE ALL SPARK

CYBERTRON

Little is known about the origins or provenance of the All Spark. Its ancient cosmic secrets remain locked away, the 'cube' as enigmatic as the strange alien symbols that adorn its fused, seamless metal surfaces. What is known is that within the All Spark lies a vast and possibly infinite reservoir of energy that has, for countless years, sustained and maintained the Transformers' home planet of Cybertron, igniting the essential 'Spark' that burns within every living Cybertronian being. But just as the All Spark had the power to create, so it also had the power – if sufficiently corrupted – to destroy. When Megatron interfaced directly with the All Spark, some part of his dark and twisted psyche was transferred to its labyrinthine consciousness, and fearing that further exposure would taint the All Spark irrevocably, turning it into a force for chaos and disorder, Optimus Prime sent it into the deepest reaches of space, far from Megatron's corrupting influence.

51

THE ALL SPARK

CYBERTRON

STATISTICS

Origin	Unknown
Location (Former)	Cybertron
Location (Current)	Earth
Associated Institutions	Sector 7
Identifying Features	Alien Hieroglyphs
Function (Former)	Life-giving Benefactor
Function (Present)	Malign Creator
Size/mass	Undefined/variable
Age	Unknown
Composition	Unknown
Current Status	Inert

'Only the All Spark can repopulate our species'

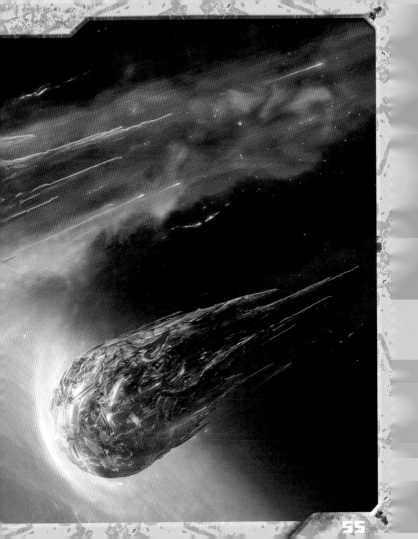

PROTOFORMS

Within every Transformer, under layers of interlocking exo-armour and chameleon plating, lies the protoform – the fluid, malleable infrastructure. Rarely seen, the protoform allows a Transformer to blend in on alien worlds or traverse vast distances of outer space. In preparation for deep space travel, the Transformer will shed its current exo-structure and then reconfigure itself into a protective transition mode, one that resembles a comet or meteor. In this form, the ravages of space and atmospheric entry can be safely weathered. Immediately upon arrival, the protoform's in-built sensors begin to seek out a suitable alternate form and, after a process known as trans-scanning, the basic form is augmented/reformatted with a new exo-structure that mimics the vehicle or life form in question. If necessary, the protoform draws on local raw materials to add extra metallic bulk. Protoforms are very tough and highly resistant to damage, capable of withstanding extremes of heat and cold and high-velocity impact.

STATISTICS

Function	Endoskeletal support
Construction	Fluid cydraulic interlock
Identifying features	Variable
Alternative Mode	Transitional carapace
Propulsion	Liquid plasma burners
Reformatting hardware	Scan-processor Mk-12
Size/Mass	Variable
Composition	Myboldeum alloy
Auxiliary system	Mineral/ore extractor
Current status	At large on earth

'Some have come to save us. Most have come to destroy us'

SAM WITWICKY

HUMAN

SAM WITWICKY

HUMAN

Though the effect of the All Spark's arrival on Earth – hundreds of thousands of years ago – would not be felt for some considerable time, the destinies of certain individuals were dramatically altered by its presence. Chief among them was Sam Witwicky, a high school student in the small town of Tranquility, Nevada. Sam's great, great grandfather, Archibald Witwicky, was the explorer who discovered Megatron, entombed under the Arctic ice, and it was his glasses (the lenses of which had been inscribed, in alien code, with the location of the All Spark) that Sam inherited on his thirteenth birthday. When, three years later, Sam listed the glasses on an online auction site, meaning to sell them to raise money for a car he wished to purchase, he drew the Decepticons to him like a magnet. Only the intervention of advance Autobot scout Bumblebee prevented his untimely demise, and the two formed a close bond that endures to this day.

SAM WITWICKY

HUMAN

STATISTICS

Played by	Shia Labeouf
Home	Tranquility, Nevada
Status	Autobot Sympathizer
Height	1.8m
Special Features	Great, great grandson of Archibald Witwicky
Likes	Cars and girls
Dislikes	Jocks
N.B.E Contact Level	High
Sector 7 Threat Rating	7

'I think... there's more to you than meets the eye'

MIKAELA BANES

HUMAN

MIKAELA BANES

The object of Sam Witwicky's (largely unspoken) affections, Mikaela Banes is a fellow student at Tranquility High. Wilful, forthright, Mikaela was a large part of the reason Sam wanted a car in the first place, but – as it turned out – instead of impressing her, he just managed to put her in mortal danger alongside him. Mikaela's father, Colin Banes, was an expert car mechanic with an unfortunate sideline in grand theft auto. Arrested and sentenced to five years in prison, Mikaela refused to give any kind of incriminating testimony against her father, resulting in a (juvenile) criminal record of her own. Mikaela clearly inherited both her father's wild streak and his knack with cars and car engines, and when push came to shove she more than proved her worth by hot-wiring a tow truck and providing some much needed mobility for the injured Bumblebee. All this adversity proved, thankfully, to be the making of Mikaela and Sam as a couple.

MIKAELA BANES

HUMAN

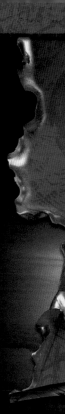

STATISTICS

Played by	Megan Fox
Home	Tranquility, Nevada
Status	Autobot Sympathizer
Height	1.7m
Special Features	Pro Car Mechanic
Likes	Fast cars and jocks
Dislikes	Cops
N.B.E Contact Level	High
Sector 7 Threat Rating	6

'I'll drive,
you shoot'

KELLER

KELLER

HUMAN

A man of power and influence, John Keller (current Secretary of Defense for the United States of America) is concerned, first and foremost, with protecting the country from external threats, be they terrestrial or extraterrestrial. Educated at Harvard, with a distinguished military career that entailed active service in Vietnam and a number of decorations for valour including a Bronze Star, Keller moved into politics in the " '80s, rising swiftly to the upper echelons of government. He doesn't suffer fools gladly, but if you're attuned to his wavelength, offering up reasoned, constructive input to the problem at hand, he's open and receptive to new ideas. Following the attack on the Soccent forward base in Qatar, Keller reached out to institutions like the Rand Corporation, seeking their expert advice. Though perhaps he and computer expert Maggie Madsen didn't get off on the best footing, Keller soon came to appreciate her intuitive way of thinking outside of the box.

KELLER

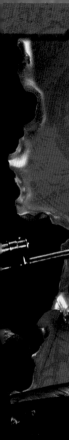

STATISTICS

Played by	**Jon Voight**
Home	**Washington, D.C.**
Status	**U.S. Secretary of Defense**
Height	**1.9m**
Special Features	**Advisor to the President**
Likes	**Free thinkers**
Dislikes	**Yes-men (women)**
N.B.E Contact Level	**Low**
Sector 7 Threat Rating	**N/A**

'This is as real as it gets'

Cpt WILLIAM LENNOX

HUMAN

Cpt WILLIAM LENNOX

HUMAN

A born leader, William Lennox worked his way up through the ranks at breathtaking speed, chalking up battle honours in the Gulf and Afghanistan. With an easy-going manner and a rough and ready sense of humour, he inspires trust and respect in those under his command. However, he's also quite the family man, with a wife, Sarah, and a new baby daughter he's yet to see in the flesh. His Special Forces unit came under attack from the Decepticon Blackout at the Soccent base in Qatar, and fought a successful rearguard action against the predatory Scorponok at a small village due east. One of his men was fatally wounded in the latter confrontation and Lennox was determined to see that those responsible be paid back in full. Returning to the U.S., he and the remainder of his unit became involved in N.B.E action at the Hoover Dam and in downtown Los Angeles... and lived to tell the tale!

Cpt WILLIAM LENNOX

HUMAN

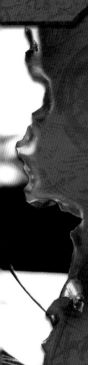

STATISTICS

Played by	Josh Duhamel
Home	Fredericksburg, Virginia
Status	Captain, U.S. Armed Forces
Height	1.9m
Special Features	Trained combat specialist
Likes	Family life
Dislikes	Decepticons
N.B.E Contact Level	High
Sector 7 Threat Rating	8

'Look at me!
You're a
soldier now'

Sgt JULIUS EPPS

HUMAN

Sgt JULIUS EPPS

HUMAN

Julius Epps was born and raised on the mean streets of East Oakland, but you wouldn't know it from his ever-cheerful demeanour and general optimism. However tough it gets or hopeless it looks, Epps remains upbeat and positive. But make no mistake, when it's called for, the smile drops away and Epps will dig in and fight to the last. He's also something of technical wizard, with natural improvisational skills and a never-say-die attitude. On the battlefield, Technical Sergeant Epps has a long list of responsibilities that include leading the members of the Special Tactics Team into uncharted, hostile territory, and once there arranging for reconnaissance, establishing attack zones and calling in air strikes, should the situation call for it. He's tough, no nonsense, and rarely phased by anything the enemy throws at him, even if the enemy in question is a giant alien robot.

Sgt JULIUS EPPS

HUMAN

STATISTICS

Played by	Tyrese Gibson
Home	Chicago, Illinois
Status	Technical Sergeant
Height	1.8m
Special Features	Technical improvisation
Likes	Hip-hop
Dislikes	Fig's Mama's alligator étouffée
N.B.E Contact Level	High
Sector 7 Threat Rating	6

'Bring the rain'

MAGGIE MADSEN

HUMAN

90

MAGGIE MADSEN

HUMAN

Born in Australia, computer whiz kid Maggie Madsen emigrated to the U.S. when she was twenty years of age, taking a job as a systems analyst with the Rand Corporation, an advanced think tank used by, among others, the U.S. government on a consultant basis. Feisty and opinionated, Maggie can't keep her mouth shut to save her life. She often tells people exactly what she thinks and then immediately regrets it, as happens the very first time she meets Defense Secretary Keller. Nevertheless, it's her instinct and insight that help unmask the true threat the world is facing when the Decepticons make their move, hacking into the Defense Department mainframe. Smart as she is, Maggie knows her limitations and acknowledges that sometimes two heads are better than one. And when she needs help, it's to cyberspace junkie Glen Whitman she goes. Together, they make an unorthodox but unstoppable team.

MAGGIE MADSEN

HUMAN

STATISTICS

Played by	Rachael Taylor
Home	Washington, D.C.
Status	Computer Analyst
Height	1.8m
Special Features	Algebraic crytpoanalysis expert
Likes	Lateral thinking
Dislikes	Red tape
N.B.E Contact Level	Low
Sector 7 Threat Rating	5

'So, asking questions would be out of the question?'

AGENT SIMMONS

HUMAN

In the case of Sector 7's (senior tactical) Agent
Simmons, giant robot hunting actually runs in the family.
To maintain its own stringent levels of internal security,
Sector 7 often recruits within the same bloodline,
and so several generations of Simmons have occupied
high-ranking positions within the Sector 7 hierarchy.
Simmons' father and grandfather both served, as did his
great grandfather, the man who supervised the removal
of Megatron from the Arctic ice and his transfer to
the under-construction Hoover Dam. The same
focused zeal personifies the current Agent
Simmons, a man who believes in just two things:
himself, and his mission to safeguard planet Earth
from alien incursion. As far as he's concerned,
anything goes. Whatever it takes to get the job
done, whoever he has to coerce or silence or
remove,' the ends justify the means. It's become
something of a personal vendetta for Agent Simmons,
him versus the N.B.E. (Non-biological Extraterrestrials).

AGENT SIMMONS

STATISTICS

Played by	John Turturro
Home	Denver, Colorado
Status	Senior Agent of Sector 7
Height	1.9m
Special Features	Great grandfather unearthed N.B.E.-1 (Megatron)
Likes	Order, Clarity
Dislikes	Unpredictable civilians
N.B.E Contact Level	High
Sector 7 Threat Rating	N/A

'See this. It's a "Do-whatever-I-want-and-get-away-with-it" badge'

JORGE FIGUEROA

HUMAN

JORGE FIGUEROA

Born and raised in the Louisiana Bayous, Jorge Figueroa ("Fig" to his friends) worked hard to make something of himself, while never forgetting his roots and his debt to a mother who brought him up alone (with three other brothers and four sisters). Whenever he gets leave, in between tours of duty with Captain Lennox's Special Tactics Team, he always goes home to see his "mama," who never tires of telling her neighbours how proud she is of her son. In the forces, Figueroa has risen to Army Chief Warrant Officer, one of the most senior ranks for a non-commissioned officer, due to his advanced level of technical and tactical competence. As such, he is responsible for managing the unit's equipment, support activities and technical systems. Following the destruction of the Soccent base in Qatar, Figueroa was at the forefront of the fighting against Decepticon predator Scorponok, a confrontation that sadly cost him his life.

JORGE FIGUEROA

HUMAN

STATISTICS

Played by	Amaury Nolasco
Home	New Orleans, Louisiana
Status	Chief Warrant Officer
Height	1.8m
Special Features	Deceased, posthumously honoured
Likes	Alligator étouffée
Dislikes	Long tours abroad
N.B.E Contact Level	Medium
Sector 7 Threat Rating	N/A

'I hit it, but this freak thing won't go down'

TOM BANACHEK

HUMAN

SECTOR 7

U.S. ARMY

TOM BANACHEK

HUMAN

Tom Banachek is a ghost. Officially, though he reports directly to the President and considers himself White House 'staff,' there's no record of his employment, no current assignment or title. Banachek is the current head of Sector 7's Advanced Research Division, an autonomous entity set up by President Hoover back in 1937. Their remit was to use the captive N.B.E-I (Megatron) and the Cube (All Spark) to reverse-engineer advanced technology that would keep America ahead in terms of its internal/external security and global market supremacy. Notable consultants affiliated to the A.R.D think-tank over the intervening years include Robert Oppenheimer (inventor of the atomic bomb), William Hayward Pickering (designer of the Explorer I space rocket) and Jack Kilby (inventor of the microchip). Banachek, a serious and committed man, currently leads the way in advanced applications of the Cube, notably channelling its power in order turn inanimate machinery into 'living' technology

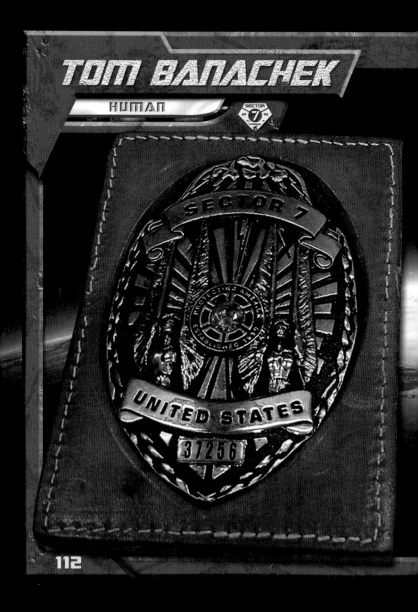

TOM BANACHEK

HUMAN

SECTOR 7

SECTOR 7

PROTECTING AMERICA ESTABLISHED 1930

UNITED STATES

37256

STATISTICS

Played by	Michael O'Neill
Home	Denver, Colorado
Status	Head of Advanced Research Division, Sector 7
Height	1.9m
Special Features	Cube (All Spark) specialist
Likes	Secrecy, deniability
Dislikes	Sharing
N.B.E Contact Level	High
Sector 7 Threat Rating	N/A

'Aliens are real, sir'

THE WITWICKYS

They say you can choose your friends, but you can't choose your family. Sam Witwicky knows all about that. His father, Ron, takes the whole idea of family really seriously, determined to instil a sense of lineage and continuance in his own offspring. When, on Sam's thirteenth birthday, Ron proudly presented his son with the dusty relics from his great grandfather Archibald's last voyage, he expected Sam to be excited, captivated or at least grateful. What he got was 'disinterested' and 'dismissive.' As for Sam's mother, Judy, she takes worrying to Olympic level and overcompensates wildly, forever 'tidying' Sam's room (i.e. looking for evidence of unsavoury pursuits). But perhaps the most troublesome relative has proven to be Sam's great, great grandfather, Archibald, whose expedition to the Arctic Circle in 1897 (and subsequent discovery, under the ice, of Megatron) set in motion a chain of events that led to Sam's imperilment at the hands of the Decepticons.

Captain
Archibald Witwicky

RON WITWICKY

HUMAN

118

STATISTICS

Played by	Kevin Dunn
Home	Tranquility, Nevada
Status	Father
Height	1.7m
Special Features	Former owner of Archibald Witwicky's glasses
Likes	Family values
Dislikes	Slackers
N.B.E Contact Level	Low
Sector 7 Threat Rating	3

'You're not getting a Porsche'

JUDY WITWICKY

STATISTICS

Played by	Julie White
Home	Tranquility, Nevada
Status	Mother
Height	1.6m
Special Features	Trainer of Mojo the chihuahua
Likes	Peace
Dislikes	Arguments
N.B.E Contact Level	Low
Sector 7 Threat Rating	2

'Sam? What are you doing in there?'

STATISTICS

Played by	William Morgan Sheppard
Home	Springfield, Missouri
Status	Explorer
Height	1.7m
Special Features	Great, great grandfather of Sam Witwicky
Likes	Long voyages
Dislikes	Asylums
N.B.E Contact Level	Medium
Sector 7 Threat Rating	2

'I didn't come all this way... to leave well alone'

SECTOR 7

HUMAN

They operate in the shadows, their existence known only to a select few high-ranking officials in US military intelligence. Their remit is to seek out and either control or eliminate extraterrestrial threats to planet Earth. Their given name is Sector 7, and they alone know and understand the scale of the threat posed by the sentient mechanical beings known as Transformers. Though the roots of Sector 7 can be traced back as far as 1869, they really came into their own in 1897, with the discovery (under the Arctic ice) of N.B.E-1 (Megatron). This major find, though, was itself eclipsed three years later, when the All Spark was uncovered in Colorado. Since then, the organization has grown and flourished (worldwide), and now commands almost unlimited funds and resources. Sector 7 is split into S7 Tactical and S7 Research & Development. The tactical division has access to highly advanced technology and weaponry.

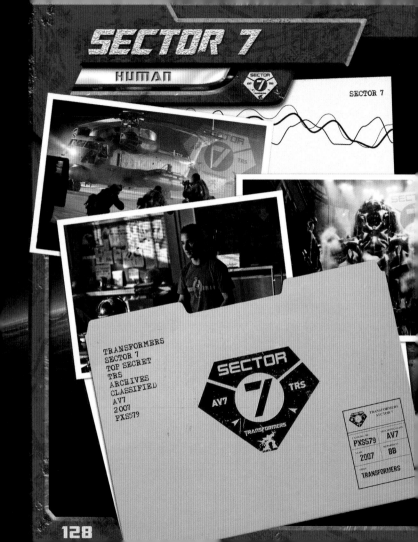

SECTOR 7

HUMAN

SECTOR 7

TRANSFORMERS
SECTOR 7
TOP SECRET
TRS
ARCHIVES
CLASSIFIED
AV7
2007
PXS579

SECTOR 7 TRS
AV7
TRANSFORMERS

	TRANSFORMERS SECTOR 7
CATALOG NO. PXS579	SECTION/CLASS AV7
YEAR 2007	REFERENCE BB
HEAD TRANSFORMERS	

STATISTICS

Function	Extraterrestrial threat management
Date of Origin	1869
Place of Origin	Boston, Massachusetts
Current Command Centre	Hoover Dam
Divisions	S7 Tactical/S7 Research & Development
Known Personnel	Agent Simmons, Tom Banachek
Ultimate Authority	The President of the USA
Jargon	N.B.E (Non-biological Extraterrestrial)

'Vigilance and Intercession'

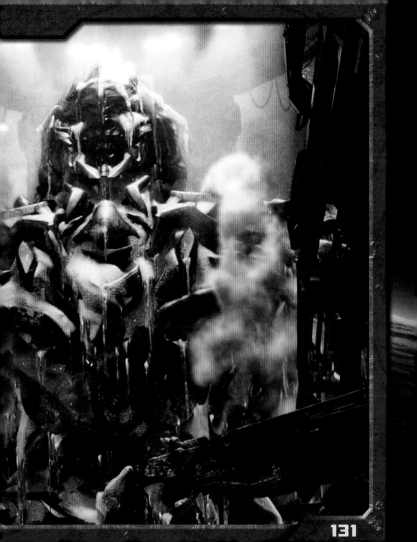

MEGATRON

DECEPTICON

Powerful, unstoppable, Megatron is a living weapon in every sense of the phrase. Once, he was the firm but even-handed Lord High Protector of Cybertron, ruling the planet alongside Optimus Prime. But that was a sham, a pretence, while Megatron bided his time, awaiting the perfect moment to strike. The All Spark, Megatron believed, was the key to unlocking buried potential within him, and via a direct interface with the ancient artefact he gained the ability to simply imagine an alternative form and make it instant reality. In doing so, he dropped his facade of cooperation and struck the first blow in a war that was to devastate Cybertron and, much later, spread to Earth. Strong beyond measure, Megatron possesses a dark matter power core of questionable origin, and he uses it to self-repair damage to his external armour and internal systems, making him very hard to injure or render inactive.

MEGATRON

DECEPTICON

Megatron's interstellar jet mode, a form he adopted directly after his interface with the All Spark, is supremely powerful, lightning fast and heavily armed. Its carbon-derivative hull absorbs energy from celestial bodies and prevents him from overheating while entering a planet's atmosphere. The vessel's top speed of Mach 3 only applies under conditions of full gravity and wind resistance. In outer space, his top speed is unknown, and he can generate a localised foldspace transition (wormhole) to traverse vast gulfs of space in an instant. Virtually soundless in flight, with a vast array of dedicated stealth features, Megatron gives little or no warning of his arrival. Then, once he is in position, he unleashes his forward barrage weapons and wing-tip lightning emitters to devastate energy positions on the ground. Megatron also possesses a matter-inversion tractor beam for snaring his prey.

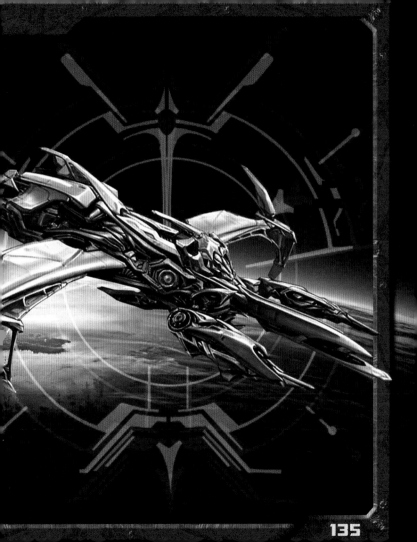

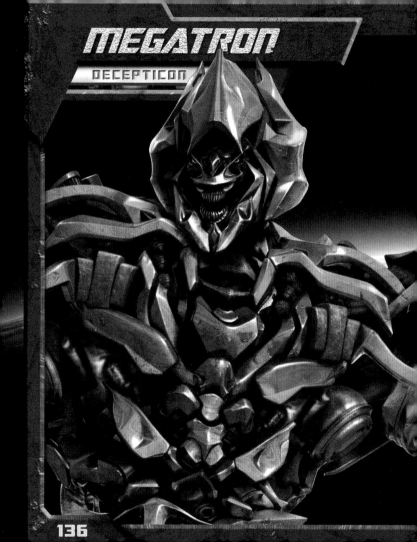

MEGATRON

STATISTICS

Alternative Mode	Interstellar Jet
Function	World-conqueror
Rank	Lord
Height	10.7m
Weight	5.7 tonnes
Power Level	5
Max. Speed	Mach 3
Engine	Plasma-injection
Primary Weapon	100-megawatt Emitters
Sector 7 Threat Rating	10+

'This world is mine!'

STARSCREAM

DECEPTICON

Never turn your back on Starscream! Cold, vicious and calculating, this Decepticon shocktrooper cares only for his own advancement and glory, and he'll go through anyone, friend or foe, to step up through the ranks. The war against the Autobots, the All Spark quest, these are not priorities in Starscream's book. It's all about looking out for number one and impressing others with whatever stratospheric headcount he can amass in any one battle. Ultimately, Starscream sees himself as supreme Decepticon Commander, but is wise enough to know that a direct challenge to Megatron's authority is out of the question. But should Megatron be otherwise removed from the equation... well, Starscream will be waiting in the wings. Trenchant and deadly in robot form, Starscream's hyper-reactive cydraulics allow him to spring at his foes with lightning speed. He never toys with those he seeks to vanquish. They are simply despatched and then he moves on.

STARSCREAM

DECEPTICON

Despite his impressive array of armaments, Starscream is rarely first into battle. He'll keep himself out of the firing line for as long as possible and let others do the hard (and dangerous) work. Then he'll sweep in and pick off any survivors. Starscream's laser-guided missiles (which can lock onto multiple targets simultaneously) are tipped with thermo-reactive warheads that burn at over 1000 degrees centigrade on impact, melting all but the densest metals. He can also access the missiles in robot mode via a shoulder-mounted flip-out launcher assembly. His chosen Earth form, that of an F-22 Raptor jet, is sleek and deadly, and he can literally brake in mid-air and use his reinforced wings as battering weapons to disable other airborne craft. Sophisticated navigational equipment allows him to fly no matter what the conditions, and he often uses thick cloud cover to sneak right up on his target before blowing them out of the sky.

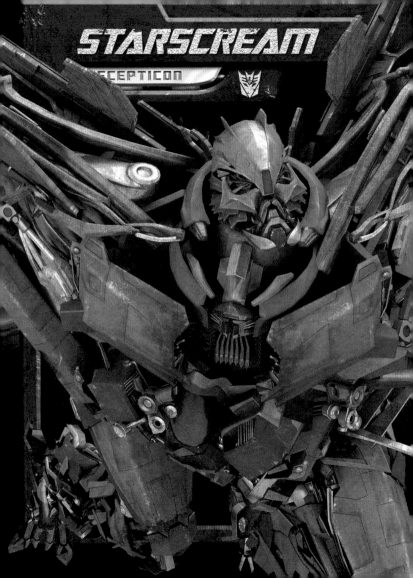

STARSCREAM

DECEPTICON

STATISTICS

Alternative Mode	F-22 Raptor
Function	Shocktrooper
Rank	Lieutentant
Height	9.4m
Weight	5.3 tonnes
Power Level	3
Max. Speed	Mach 3.4
Engine	35000lb Thrust-class (x2)
Primary Weapon	Cluster Dispersal Launcher
Sector 7 Threat Rating	8

'I rule
the skies!'

BARRICADE

BARRICADE

DECEPTICON

Fast and furious, that's Barricade in a nutshell. This is one 'bot with a serious need for speed, a trait that inevitably sees him way out in front of every other Decepticon on the battlefield. Though he's extremely adept and proficient at disguise and infiltration, often selecting the optimum alternate form to allow him to go wherever he wants, unchallenged, it's the bit he really doesn't like. Barricade would rather be up front and up close and personal, inflicting as much pain and distress as possible. It's Barricade's sheer willingness to throw himself headlong into any mission or battle that has made him indispensable to Megatron and, in the process, has made an enemy out of Starscream. In robot mode, Barricade is able to deflect incoming fire with a reactive defence system. He can switch through a variety of different fields of vision in order to probe for weaknesses in an opponent's armature

BARRICADE

DECEPTICON

Needing fast access to information and the ability to go places – fast, of course – where the presence of other vehicle makes might raise suspicion, Barricade reconfigured his protoform into a clone of a Saleen Mustang police cruiser. But though the disguise was note perfect, Barricade couldn't resist a little flourish of his own, replacing the standard 'to protect and serve' tag with 'to punish and enslave.' Confirming his suspicion that humans were an ignorant lot, no one noticed. Fast, direct, with forward reinforced ramming bars, Barricade took full advantage of his disguise, forcibly removing obstacles from his path in his quest to find Sam Witwicky, whom he suspected unwittingly held the key to the location of the All Spark. Barricade can, in certain circumstances, initiate a super-burn sequence, going from zero to 200mph in point six of a second, however this seriously depletes his available fuel.

BARRICADE

STATISTICS

Alternative Mode	Saleen Mustang
Function	Vanguard Trooper
Rank	Sub-lieutenant
Height	5m
Weight	2.2 tonnes
Power Level	3
Max. Speed	300mph
Engine	550hp
Primary Weapon	Gyro-flight Blades
Sector 7 Threat Rating	8

'When the time is ripe, we shall reveal ourselves!'

BLACKOUT

DECEPTICON

154

BLACKOUT

Blackout likes to soften up his enemies before he finally engages them in combat. Self-preservation is high on his list of priorities – largely because he's one of the most lightly armoured Decepticons – and so Blackout first sows disarray, misdirection and chaos, a large slice of pandemonium designed distract and otherwise occupy the enemy. Then, when they least expect it, he strikes – hard and fast. There's always a huge amount of collateral damage when Blackout's on the case, and he's a specialist at blowing things up and making a big, big noise. Often positioned by Megatron at the forefront of any attack, Blackout responded by surrounding himself with his own personal drone troopers, who act much like aerial chaff, drawing the enemy fire. In robot mode, Blackout generally announces his presence with a piercing, disorienting sonic shriek that attacks both electrical systems and human nervous systems.

BLACKOUT

DECEPTICON

Manoeuvrability is key to Blackout's chosen modus operandi. His secondary mode has got to be capable of direct attack and fast evasive action, qualities that the MH-53 helicopter has in abundance. In this form, Blackout can climb or dive steeply at a moment's notice, which suits his preferred tactic of making his approach at high altitude and then plunging into a steep attack dive. He thrives in adverse weather conditions that would ground a normal MH-53, using gale force winds, clouds and even snow as cover, emerging from the heart of the storm to rain destruction down on enemy positions. Once he's in range, Blackout unleashes his sonic barrage attack, following up immediately with concussion blasts and machine gun fire. In airborne mode, Blackout can access sophisticated thermal imagers that reveal the area below in minute detail, and he's often despatched to ferret out concealed enemy forces laying in wait.

BLACKOUT

DECEPTICON

STATISTICS

Alternative Mode	MH-53 Helicopter
Function	Vanguard Trooper
Rank	Sub-lieutenant
Height	10.2m
Weight	2.9 tonnes
Power Level	2
Max. Speed	800mph
Engine	7000shp (x2)
Primary Weapon	Sonic Barrage Cannon
Sector 7 Threat Rating	7

'My allies are chaos, confusion and carnage!'

BONECRUSHER

DECEPTICON

BONECRUSHER

DECEPTICON

No one knows hate quite like Bonecrusher, or so he likes to think. He hates everything: Autobots, humans, his fellow Decepticons, even himself! His hunched, misshapen robot form is, he believes, a reflection of his inner ugliness. He even hates Megatron, but is wise enough never to let it show. Of course, it's Bonecrusher's enemies who bear the brunt of all this self-hatred and bitterness, as he takes out his anger and frustration on them. He'll take on anyone, the bigger the better. Optimus Prime? Bring him on! Mean, vicious, Bonecrusher is utterly dedicated to the art of war. While his opponents are still formulating their strategy, Bonecrusher strikes. He's a master of fighting dirty, targeting an opponent's most, er, vulnerable areas. In robot mode, Bonecrusher can accelerate from standing to 50mph in just two seconds, using disguised (traction-free) roller features in his feet.

BONECRUSHER

DECEPTICON

In vehicular mode, Bonecrusher is a modified Buffalo MPCV mine clearer, his jointed, claw mechanism a multi-function weapon and probe. The carbon-tungsten tipped claws can tear through armour plating, stone and even energy fields. His 360-degree extendable crane arm can be used to wreak havoc left, right and centre, and can separate into two independent units, protecting either flank. The claw itself has a rotating ball joint, enabling it to spin at high speed like whirling rotor blades. In this attack mode, there's very little that isn't shredded instantly on contact, and in a pursuit situation the extra distance enabled by the extension of the crane arm can be decisive. The claws are loaded with sensitive probes, which when inserted in the ground can detect the presence of buried explosive devices and disarm/remove them. In military campaigns, Bonecrusher is usually deployed ahead of the ground forces to clear a safe path for them.

BONECRUSHER

DECEPTICON

STATISTICS

Alternative Mode	Buffalo MPCV
Function	Shocktrooper
Rank	Sub-lieutenant
Height	7.7m
Weight	1.9 tonnes
Power Level	3
Max. Speed	230mph
Engine	260hp
Primary Weapon	Claw-arm
Sector 7 Threat Rating	8

'War and me
go together.
We're both ugly'

DEVASTATOR

DEVASTATOR

DECEPTICON

It's rumoured that Devastator thinks only of war and destruction, but whether that's due to focus or a limited amount of hard drive space is open to conjecture. Certainly Devastator could never be accused of being the sharpest tool in Megatron's box. He's monosyllabic and slow to process information, a lumbering brute who thinks largely with his fists and expresses himself by blowing stuff up. He's survived this long not because of his battle acumen or keen instinct for self-preservation (of which he has neither) but because he's just very hard to kill. With three layers of reinforced and compacted armour plating and shock-displacement buffers, nothing much short of a nuke can crack his casing. He also carries an inordinate amount of weaponry, from surface-to-air rocket launcher pods to chain guns to seismic land mines, and loves to use it. For close combat, a spring-loaded, twelve-foot tungsten bayonet can be deployed.

The appearance of a (modified) MI-AI Abrams tank suits Devastator down to the ground. His angular, reflective armour is designed to deceive the eye, making him appear slightly to the right of where he actually is. He can fire up to twenty (non-nuclear) 'Thor' missiles from his gun turret, one after the other if necessary (with a reload time of only point eight of a second) and (from the same turret) a concentrated pulse jet, with an explosive force equal to 2000lbs of TNT. A sub-turret fires surface-to-air optical command guided warheads. Side-mounted small arms barrels can disgorge 200 rounds per second and rear-mounted mortar launchers round off his main vehicle mode arsenal. By far the slowest of the Decepticons, Devastator is often let loose in advance of the main tactical force, to do as much damage as possible. Devastator also possesses a forward minesweeper 'comb.'

OPE

DEVASTATOR

DECEPTICON

STATISTICS

Alternative Mode	M1-A1 Abrams Tank
Function	Trooper
Rank	Private
Height	7.6m
Weight	12 tonnes
Power Level	4
Max. Speed	110mph
Engine	Gas Turbine
Primary Weapon	Rocket Launcher
Sector 7 Threat Rating	8

'If it moves,
crush it'

FRENZY

DECEPTICON

FRENZY

DECEPTICON

Small, nimble, multi-jointed and deadly, Frenzy is a master of disguise, switching his secondary form as often as most humans change their socks. He can be anything from a boom box to a PDA to a mobile phone, and in those guises go anywhere unnoticed, gaining access to any and all restricted areas. Perfect for deep cover infiltration missions, Frenzy goes about his work with a gleeful zeal, utterly contemptuous of those on whom he spies. He never gives up, and his de-centralized nervous system means that even if he sustains critical injuries, he can continue to function. Essentially, every little bit of him is alive... and deadly. For despite his diminutive size, Frenzy has a lethal array of offensive options, including a sonic shockwave, a laser cutter and his chest-mounted disc-slinger, which launches circular discs with razor sharp barbs, one at a time or in a rapid-fire sequence.

FRENZY

STATISTICS

Alternative Mode	Various
Function	Infiltration
Rank	Trooper
Height	1.4m
Weight	110kg
Power Level	1
Max. Speed	N/A
Engine	N/A
Primary Weapon	Disc Slinger
Sector 7 Threat Rating	5

'Anytime,
anywhere,
anything!'

SCORPONOK

DECEPTICON

SCORPONOK

DECEPTICON

Though small, Scorponok is every bit as lethal as
Decepticons three or four times his size. His stinger
(mounted in his tail) fires a cyber-venom bolt capable
of paralysis and even, if a critical system is infected,
death. He also comes with an array of ballistic
options, including cluster bombs and mortar shells.
No one quite knows if Scorponok possesses a rudimentary
intelligence or functions purely on instinct, like a drone.
There's a suspicion there's a lot more to him than meets
the eye, and that it's his way of making sure friend and
foe alike underestimate him. Scorponok's
chameleon mesh armour plates
allow him to hitch a ride on
larger Decepticons and blend
in with their own disguise.
Often, he and Blackout work
as a team. Adept at digging
tunnels with his powerful forward
pincers, which can spin at 1500rpm,
Scorponok operates largely underground.

SCORPONOK

DECEPTICON

STATISTICS

Alternative Mode	n/A
Function	Hunter
Rank	n/A
Height	2.6m
Weight	0.6 Tonnes
Power Level	2
Max. Speed	n/A
Engine	n/A
Primary Weapon	Stinger
Sector 7 Threat Rating	5

'What in God's name is that?'

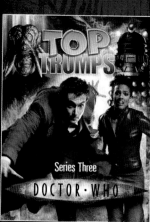
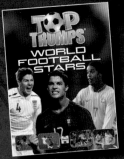

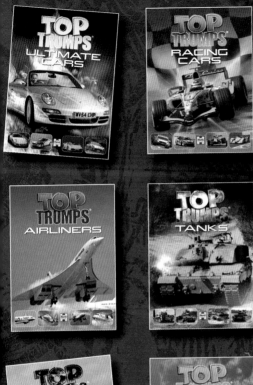